ECOMING
creative

BECOMING
thoughtful

BECOMING
strong

D0090383

ECOMING
inspired

BECOMING
honest

BECOMING
open

ECOMING
urposeful

BECOMING
driven

BECOMING
creative

ECOMING
helpful

BECOMING
happy

BECOMING
curious

ECOMING
ecure

BECOMING
brave

BECOMING
thankful

I AM BECOMING

Your story is what you have,
what you will always have.
It is something to own.

This story belongs to

_____

(Me)

Becoming
isn't about arriving
somewhere or
achieving a certain
aim. It's forward
motion, a means
of evolving,
a way to reach
continuously
toward a better self.

A NOTE FROM MICHELLE

After my memoir was published, I heard a similar reaction from a lot of people—strangers, friends, and family alike. They said, "I just can't believe you remembered that much." It's a comment that usually gave me a bit of a chuckle, because when I think back to the process of reflecting for my memoir, what I remember most is the feeling of grasping at memories that were just barely out of my reach. *What was her name? Did I make that decision before or after that talk with Barack? Which state was that campaign event in?*

I'd only kept a journal for a short period of my life, for a couple of years during my late twenties as I was getting more serious with Barack and contemplating a new career. It was a tumultuous time filled with change, and I found that dedicating time to writing my thoughts down helped me navigate all the transitions. Then I put it away and didn't pick it up again until I began writing my memoir. Instantly, I was transported back to that earlier version of myself, with all the warmth, heartbreak, and frustration flooding in.

The experience left me asking myself, "Why didn't I journal more?" The answer, like for so many of you, I'm sure, was that I simply got busy. I switched careers. I got married. I had children. Somewhere along the line, I ended up in ball gowns at the White House, however that happened.

Looking back, I wish I'd taken more time to write down what I was thinking and feeling. I didn't journal much because I talked myself out of it—journaling can feel a little intimidating and layered with implication, the idea being that once you put pen to paper, your thoughts have extra weight and meaning.

What I recognize now, though, is far more simple: We don't have to remember everything. But everything we remember has value.

You don't have to write in poetry or wait for some lightning-bolt epiphany. You don't have to journal every day, and you certainly don't have to feel like you have anything important to say. You might write down something as mundane as the sound of an ice scraper on a windshield on a freezing-cold Chicago morning. The whiff of Pine-Sol in the house after spring cleaning. The ride home from the airport in your mother's car. Your to-do list for the next day, even. One of my favorite entries recounted an otherwise uneventful night at a neighborhood restaurant where an old man punched the perfect playlist into a jukebox.

Just remember that everything matters—the sounds and the smells, the laughs and the pain—because in the end, it's all a part of your story. I hope you'll use this journal to write down your experiences, thoughts, and feelings, in all their imperfections, and without judgment. This isn't an exercise to sugarcoat your experiences, or write down something different from what you actually feel, or try to will yourself toward some perfect outcome. Because the beauty of life is that an experience you have today might feel totally different after a few months, or years, or decades. You might return to these pages and recognize parts of yourself that you can't even see today, which is especially true for those of you who are still in the early stages of your journeys, when the joys and hurt can sometimes feel too fresh, too raw. Writing is a way to process, to understand, to grow, and yes, to remember.

That's perhaps the most fundamental part of becoming: seeing this collection of stories that you'll write and embracing them for what they are—yours.

Much love,

Michelle Obama

If you don't see that your story matters, chances are no one else will either. So even though it isn't always easy, it's important for you to find the strength to share your truth. Because the world needs to hear it.

What's your story and
how have you learned
to embrace it?

Where did your story
take a sudden turn?

BECOMING

Do you have any favorite quotes? Capture three of them here.

Describe your
proudest moment
in the fullest detail
possible.

I was raised to be
confident and see
no limits, to believe
I could go after
and get absolutely
anything I wanted.
And I wanted
everything . . .

What do you want? List ten things you want for yourself. For each item,
write one simple step toward making that wish come true.

1. _____

   _____

2. _____

   _____

3. _____

   _____

4. _____

   _____

5. _____

   _____

6. _____

   _____

7. _____

   _____

8. _____

   _____

9. _____

   _____

10. _____

   _____

Describe your
childhood home.
What are some of
the details that stand
out the most? What
made your home
different from your
friends' homes?

Describe your home today. How is it different from your friends' homes? What do you love about it the most?

DATE   /   /

I had nothing or I had everything. It depends on which way you want to tell it.

Where we come from has such a strong effect on the person we are. Describe the neighborhood you grew up in. What was special about it? What was challenging? How did it shape who you are today?

List five favorite family dishes.

1

2

3

4

5

Describe a memorable dinner. What did you eat? Did you eat at home or somewhere else?

BECOMING

What did you do as a
child when school let
out for the summer?

What activities did you previously pursue but don't have time for now? How can you get back to them again?

BECOMING

If you could have a
conversation with
a loved one who
has passed away,
what would you ask
him or her?

Where did your
ancestors come from
and what challenges
did they face?

BECOMING

If there's one thing I've learned in life, it's the power of using your own voice.

Write about a time when you spoke your truth to others. How did it make you feel? What did you learn?

What kind of person
do you want to
become?

How do you want
to contribute to
the world? What
is one small step
you can take this
year to further that
contribution?

Have courage this month to share a little more of your story with someone else. Ask them about theirs. What did you learn about yourself? What did you learn about this person?

There's power in allowing yourself to be known and heard, in owning your unique story, in using your authentic voice. And there's grace in being willing to know and hear others. This, for me, is how we become.

What are the greatest
lessons you learned
as a child?

My family was my world, the center of everything.

What does family mean to you?

In as much detail
as possible, capture
one favorite memory
you've created with
your loved ones.

Describe your perfect day—beginning with breakfast and ending with dinner.

Write a letter to your
teenage self, giving
advice and revealing
what the future holds.

Write a letter to your
future self, outlining
your expectations for
the years to come.

What's the most spontaneous thing you have ever done?

_____

_____

_____

_____

_____

_____

_____

_____

_____

_____

_____

_____

_____

_____

_____

_____

_____

_____

What were the ten biggest things that happened to you this month?

1. _____

2. _____

3. _____

4. _____

5. _____

6. _____

7. _____

8. _____

9. _____

10. _____

I was female, black,
and strong, which
to certain people,
maintaining a certain
mind-set, translated only
to "angry." It was another
damaging cliché, one
that's been forever used to
sweep minority women
to the perimeter of every
room, an unconscious
signal not to listen to
what we've got to say.

Have you ever felt
subject to a cliché?
How did you react?

Look outside a
window in your home.
Write down what
you see.

What was the biggest news headline on the day you were born? Is it something that is still relevant today?

BECOMING

What was the last
great book you read?
What did you learn
from it?

One of the first books that
I loved and read cover to
cover in one day . . . was a
book called *Song of Solomon*
by Toni Morrison. And that
book helped me love reading,
because before then reading
was kind of like something
you did when you had to do it.
But that book, it grabbed me
and pulled me and I just kept
reading and kept reading. . . .
There are many, many other
books that I've read like that
over the years, but *Song of
Solomon* was my first one.

List ten fun things you like to do.

1. _____

_____

2. _____

_____

3. _____

_____

4. _____

_____

5. _____

_____

6. _____

_____

7. _____

_____

8. _____

_____

9. _____

_____

10. _____

_____

What is your most prized possession and how did you come to own it?

Failure is a
feeling long before
it becomes an
actual result.
It's vulnerability
that breeds with
self-doubt and then
is escalated,
often deliberately,
by fear.

What can you do—as an individual, parent, or
community member—to help break a cycle of
fear and failure?

Pick a favorite photo
and write a story
describing what you
see.

Who is the happiest
person you know?
What do you think
brings them joy?

BECOMING

In seeking out
new perspectives
and reaching outside
of our comfort
zones, we can
discover more about
ourselves.

If you could travel anywhere, where would
you go and what would you do?

Think back to your childhood when you would visit grandparents or other elders. Capture one specific memory from those visits in the fullest detail possible, including the sights, sounds, and smells.

How have those elders
left a mark on you?

List ten favorite vegetables and how you like to prepare them.

1. _____

_____

2. _____

_____

3. _____

_____

4. _____

_____

5. _____

_____

6. _____

_____

7. _____

_____

8. _____

_____

9. _____

_____

10. _____

_____

I now knew that
strawberries were at
their most succulent
in June, that darker-
leaf lettuces had the
most nutrients, and
that it wasn't so hard
to make kale chips
in the oven.

How does nature
nourish you?

How do you celebrate
the holidays? What
traditions does your
family hold dear?

Describe a memorable
holiday—whether
recently or in the past.
Where were you? Who
was there? What food
was served?

You don't really know how attached you are until you move away, until you've experienced what it means to be dislodged, a cork floating on the ocean of another place.

When were you last flung into new or uncomfortable terrain? How did this sudden change affect you? What value did it bring to your life?

Kids will invest more when they feel they're being invested in.

List five people who invested in you
when you were a child.

1

2

3

4

5

Choose one person from your list on the opposite page and describe how his or her support manifested in your accomplishments today.

How did you get to
school every day when
you were young?

Who was the most
influential teacher
when you were
little? How did this
person leave such an
impression?

What has been your
greatest sacrifice?

I have a habit that has
sustained me for life:
keeping a close and
high-spirited council of
girlfriends—a safe harbor
of female wisdom.

List three people who contribute
to your circle of strength. Next to
each person's name, describe why
he or she is so dependable.

2

3

Create a playlist of ten songs that you could listen to on repeat.

1. _____

_____

2. _____

_____

3. _____

_____

4. _____

_____

5. _____

_____

6. _____

_____

7. _____

_____

8. _____

_____

9. _____

_____

10. _____

_____

Music has
always been
a defining part
of who I've
become.

A BECOMING PLAYLIST

1. "Ain't No Mountain High Enough," Marvin Gaye and Tammi Terrell

2. "The Way You Do the Things You Do," The Temptations

3. "Dancing in the Street," Martha Reeves & the Vandellas

4. "Please, Mr. Postman," The Marvelettes

5. "This Old Heart of Mine (Is Weak for You)," The Isley Brothers

6. "Ain't Nothing Like the Real Thing," Marvin Gaye and Tammi Terrell

7. "Baby Love," The Supremes

8. "It's the Same Old Song," Four Tops

9. "Just My Imagination (Running Away with Me)," The Temptations

10. "Signed, Sealed, Delivered (I'm Yours)," Stevie Wonder

11. "I Heard It Through the Grapevine," Gladys Knight & the Pips

12. "My Guy," Mary Wells

13. "It Takes Two," Marvin Gaye and Kim Weston

14. "I Can't Help Myself (Sugar Pie, Honey Bunch)," Four Tops

15. "Who's Loving You," The Jackson 5

16. "Beauty Is Only Skin Deep," The Temptations

17. "The Tracks of My Tears," Smokey Robinson & the Miracles

18. "For Once in My Life," Stevie Wonder

19. "Baby, I'm for Real," The Originals

20. "Reach Out I'll Be There," Four Tops

21. "What's Going On," Marvin Gaye

22. "Mercy Me (The Ecology)," Marvin Gaye

23. "As," Stevie Wonder

24. "Color," Zhané

25. "I Love Your Smile," Shanice

26. "Treat Her Like a Lady," The Temptations

27. "Zoom," Commodores

28. "The Truth," India.Arie

29. "Didn't Cha Know," Erykah Badu

30. "My Cherie Amour," Stevie Wonder

31. "Woman's World," BJ the Chicago Kid

32. "I'm Coming Out," Diana Ross

33. "Video," India.Arie

34. "Square Biz," Teena Marie

35. "Rhythm of the Night," DeBarge

36. "You and I," Rick James

37. "Someday We'll Be Together," Diana Ross & the Supremes

38. "Feel So Good," Perri

I've learned that it's harder to hate up close.

Describe a recent conversation you had with someone who did not share your history or perspective. How did you navigate the conversation?

What kind of
childhood did
your parents or
grandparents have?
How was it different
from and similar to
your own?

Your story is the most powerful part of who you are—the struggles, failures, successes, and everything in between. Remember always to stay open to new experiences and never let the doubters get in the way.

List one struggle, one failure, and one success you've encountered in your life. What did you learn from each?

A STRUGGLE:

_____

_____

_____

_____

_____

A FAILURE:

_____

_____

_____

_____

_____

A SUCCESS:

_____

_____

_____

_____

_____

Have you spent time
in the military, or know
someone who has?
What does it mean
to you to serve your
country?

How would you
describe yourself to
someone who does
not know you?

BECOMING

Becoming requires equal parts patience and rigor.

Describe a time when patience and rigor contributed to your own self-love and growth.

Write about a specific experience when someone dislodged a dream of yours by trying to lower your expectations. How did it make you feel? How did you try to overcome that obstacle?

List five ways that person was wrong.

1

2

3

4

5

When was your last
good cry, and how did
you feel afterward?

How do you look after
yourself after you've
had a bad day?

A transition
is exactly that—
a passage to
something new.

What transition are you going through right now?
Do you feel ready for it?

What was the best
TV show you saw as
a kid? What are you
watching now?

Who is your favorite
TV show character
and what about them
appeals to you?

BECOMING

Think of an endeavor you recently
embarked upon—one which may have
felt new, exciting, and perhaps a bit scary.
List three of your attributes that made you
uniquely qualified for the challenge.

2

3

If you could travel
back in time and
give yourself advice
before you took on
a challenge, what
would you say?

How have your beliefs
changed over the
years? How have they
remained the same?

Reflect on your
greatest struggle.
What was it and
how did you grow
from it?

Everyone on
earth is carrying
around an unseen
history, and that
alone deserves some
tolerance.

What major historical events affected your
family—whether in the distant past or more
recently?

What role does
religion or spirituality
play in your life?

Write about a time
when you felt carefree.

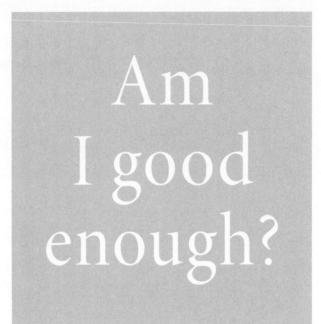

Am
I good
enough?

Yes
I am.

List ten reasons you are a special and worthy person. Look back at this list whenever you are in doubt. You are always good enough!

1. _____

_____

2. _____

_____

3. _____

_____

4. _____

_____

5. _____

_____

6. _____

_____

7. _____

_____

8. _____

_____

9. _____

_____

10. _____

_____

Write a thank-you
letter to someone
you love.

How do you connect
with your community?

Describe your community and how it has evolved over the past decade.

List five changes you wish a civic leader would take on that would greatly affect your community for the better.

1

2

3

4

5

List your greatest gifts. Remember to embrace them and lay them on the table with pride!

1. _____

_____

2. _____

_____

3. _____

_____

4. _____

_____

5. _____

_____

6. _____

_____

7. _____

_____

8. _____

_____

9. _____

_____

10. _____

_____

How do you define the word *leader*? Have you ever considered taking on a leadership role? Why or why not?

Self-doubt doesn't make the feelings any less difficult in the moment, but in the end, it can actually be useful, as long as we don't let it overwhelm the way we think about ourselves.

What worries about yourself have you had that proved to be untrue? What methods do you use when faced with self-doubt?

So many of us go
through life with
our stories hidden,
feeling ashamed
or afraid when our
whole truth doesn't
live up to some
established ideal . . .
That is, until
someone dares to
start telling that
story differently.

Describe someone
you know who was
brave enough to
tell their story. How
did it change your
perception of them?
How did it change
your perception of
yourself?

How do you mark the
seasons? What is your
favorite month of the
year?

Do you embrace
change in your own
life? Why or why not?

To me, the magic is in the learning.

What skills or lessons have you sought to learn as an adult? How does learning bring about change in your life today?

DATE / /

BECOMING

What trailblazer
throughout history
has shaped you the
most? If you could
meet this person,
what questions
would you ask?

What legacy do you
want to leave behind?

We were planting seeds of change, the fruit of which we might never see. We had to be patient.

List five tiny victories you accomplished this week.

1

2

3

4

5

Change happens from the ground up. What is one small thing you
can do this week to bring about new change in your life or in the life
of someone else?

BECOMING

If you don't get out there and define yourself, you'll be quickly and inaccurately defined by others.

How have others tried to define you in the past and how do their perceptions differ from the person you know you are?

Write about someone outside your family who feels like a family member. What do you love about them the most?

The important parts
of my story, I was
realizing, lay less in
the surface value of my
accomplishments and
more in what undergirded
them—the many small
ways I'd been buttressed
over the years, and the
people who'd helped build
my confidence over time.

Who are your mentors and how do you cultivate
those relationships?

How often do you get together with your friends, and what do you like to do? Is it enough?

List your ten favorite movies.

1. _____

_____

2. _____

_____

3. _____

_____

4. _____

_____

5. _____

_____

6. _____

_____

7. _____

_____

8. _____

_____

9. _____

_____

10. _____

_____

How do you give back
to your community?

How have you been
able to create change
in the lives of other
people?

If you were asked to give a commencement speech, what advice would you offer the graduates?

What happened in your life today? List five things that went well.

What does self-care
mean to you? How
can you make more
time for taking care
of yourself?

Who do you care for
in your family? How
does that relationship
help define you?

Coexisting with
Barack's strong sense
of purpose . . .
was something
to which I had to
adjust, not because
he flaunted it,
exactly, but because
it was so alive.

What gives you purpose? Who else in your life
shares your resolve?

Have you experienced
loss? How did it shape
your life?

Write about the
last moment you
remember being truly
at peace. Where were
you? What were you
doing? How can you
tap into that feeling
again?

BECOMING

When is the last time you felt you might be on the wrong path even though the world thought you were doing exactly the right thing? What did you decide to do?

List the ten most important social issues you feel need attending to.

1. _____

_____

2. _____

_____

3. _____

_____

4. _____

_____

5. _____

_____

6. _____

_____

7. _____

_____

8. _____

_____

9. _____

_____

10. _____

_____

When they go low, we go high.

How do you put this phrase into practice?

Who was your first
love?

How does your family
handle the pressures
of the outside world?

Have you ever
embraced ambitions
that put you at odds
with the people
you love and trust
the most? How did
you straddle those
different worlds?

If you could find more
time to do what you love,
what would you do?

BECOMING

I wanted to have a
work life and a home life,
but with some promise
that one would never fully
squelch the other.
I hoped to be exactly like
my own mother and
at the same time nothing
like her at all. It was an
odd and confounding
thing to ponder.
Could I have everything?
Would I have everything?
I had no idea.

How do you balance
the competing worlds
of your home life and
work life?

BECOMING

List ten outings you've been on with your family.

1. _____

_____

2. _____

_____

3. _____

_____

4. _____

_____

5. _____

_____

6. _____

_____

7. _____

_____

8. _____

_____

9. _____

_____

10. _____

_____

Pick one outing from your list and dig a little deeper: what did you do, where did you go, and who went with you?

Who or what are you
grateful for?

How do you express
your gratitude?

When have you had to
swerve in life? How did
it help you?

How do you stay
centered?

BECOMING

What is your favorite way to unwind from a particularly demanding day?

What inspires you? List the first ten things that come to mind.

1. _____

_____

2. _____

_____

3. _____

_____

4. _____

_____

5. _____

_____

6. _____

_____

7. _____

_____

8. _____

_____

9. _____

_____

10. _____

_____

The most successful people I know have figured out how to live with criticism, to lean on the people who believe in them, and to push onward with their goals.

Reflect on one person you know who has overcome obstacles to accomplish their goals. How do you think they did it? What have you learned from their journey?

Describe a time when
you had to speak up
for yourself. What gave
you the courage? What
stood in your way?

Have you ever felt
the need to speak
up for someone else?
Describe the situation
and the outcome.

Who is your role
model? How has that
person shaped you?

Who looks up to you?
How do you nurture
that person's spark?

What's the best part of your morning routine?

List five things you do to unwind from the day.

Capture a favorite
family recipe here.
How is it unique?

Where did your name
come from and how
has it influenced
the person you've
become?

BECOMING

How do you bring
your own history,
culture, and
experiences into
spaces where they
never existed?

If you could rewrite
history books, what
would you add that
was left out?

Describe the world
of your dreams. What
changes—whether
on a local, national,
or global level—do
you wish to see?

People of all backgrounds, skin colors, and political persuasions can relate to feeling uncertain or overwhelmed. We've all been a little frustrated by the slow, frustrating growth necessary to get where we want to go.

Describe a specific
place that holds
important meaning
to your family.

If you had to choose, who is the most precious person in your life? How did you meet this person and what do you think your future together holds?

What were five books you loved as a child?

1

2

3

4

5

Describe someone in your life who is truly wise.

BECOMING

Use this space to write
a letter to someone
you haven't seen in a
long time, updating
him or her on what's
happened in your
life since you last saw
each other.

Use this space to
capture your favorite
family sayings along
with who said them
and what they mean
to you.

In my life so far, I'd worn very few gowns, but Jason Wu's creation performed a potent little miracle, making me feel soft and beautiful and open again, just as I began to think I had nothing of myself left to show.

List ten items of clothing you loved along with when and where you wore them.

1. _____

_____

2. _____

_____

3. _____

_____

4. _____

_____

5. _____

_____

6. _____

_____

7. _____

_____

8. _____

_____

9. _____

_____

10. _____

_____

Education has
been the primary
instrument of
change in my own
life, my lever upward
in the world.

What role has education—whether formal or
informal—played in your life?

In as much detail as possible, describe one of your favorite childhood memories.

List ten things you noticed on your way home today that no one else may have noticed.

1. _____

2. _____

3. _____

4. _____

5. _____

6. _____

7. _____

8. _____

9. _____

10. _____

Spend an evening
or afternoon without
looking at social
media or the news.
How did it feel to
unplug even for just a
short amount of time?

When your extended
family gets together,
what do you do?

I was lucky to have parents, teachers, and mentors who'd fed me with a consistent, simple message:

You matter.

Who makes you feel like you matter? How do they let you know?

What do you like to do to stay healthy?

List three new hobbies you'd like to learn to do. What about each of them appeals to you?

My father loved any excuse to drive. He was devoted to his car, a bronze-colored two-door Buick Electra 225, which he referred to with pride as "the Deuce and a Quarter."

Describe your family car or other mode of transportation you took as a child. Capture the sounds and smells.

What's the longest
road trip you've ever
been on?

What would make
your neighborhood a
better place?

Kids know at a very young age when they're being devalued.

How do you make the children in your life feel valued?

What keeps you up at
night?

How has this year
been different from
last year?

DATE   /   /

What five things do you want to have accomplished by the end of the month?

1

2

3

4

5

Close this journal, shut your eyes, and take ten deep breaths. Write down how you feel.

BECOMING

Think of a time when
you gave away some-
thing you loved. What
did you give away
and why?

When was the last
time you saw the
sunset? What were you
doing at the time?

Becoming is never giving up on the idea that there's more growing to be done.

What does the idea of "becoming" mean to you?

CLARKSON POTTER is a trademark and POTTER with colophon
is a registered trademark of Penguin Random House LLC.

Selected material originally appeared in *Becoming* by Michelle
Obama, published by Crown, an imprint of Penguin Random
House LLC, New York, in 2018.

ISBN 978-0-593-13912-7

Printed in the United States of America

Design by Danielle Deschenes

10 9 8 7 6 5 4 3 2 1

First Edition